Instructions on page 2.

D1567316

HELPFUL HINTS FOR EMBROIDERY

Fabrics: Medium-weight linen for embroidery is easy to work with, but you can use any kind of fabric, too. Choose the most suitable fabric for the purpose.

Threads: Six-strand embroidery floss, No. 25 is mostly used. Pearl cotton, coton à broder, gold and silver lamé threads, yarns, etc. are also used.

Frames: Use an embroidery frame for stretching the fabric evenly and for working even stitches. You may work embroidery without using a frame, but take care not to pull thread too tight or not to deform the fabric.

How to transfer designs: Place the fabric to be embroidered on the working board with the right side up. Place a piece of carbon paper on the embroidery area of the fabric with the carbon side down. Use a carbon similar in color to the fabric. Place a piece of tracing paper with designs and cellophane on top. Pin all the layers together at corners and trace with a stylus pen.

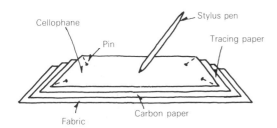

Needles: Needles from size three to ten are used for French embroidery. The bigger the number, the finer and shorter the needle. Choose the most suitable needle for the fabric and thread.

Fabric, Thread and Needle Chart:

Fabrics	Needles	Threads
Heavy-weight	No. 3·No. 4	4~6 strands
Medium-weight	No. 5	3 strands
Light-weight	No. 6~No. 10	1 strand·2 strands

Starting and Ending: Instead of making a knot at the end of thread, leave 5—6cm (2″-2⅜″) of thread at the starting point. After finishing embroidery, weave that thread into the stitches, 2—3cm (¾″-1¼″) on the wrong side. Cut off extra thread. At the end of the stitches, weave the remaining thread in the same way.

How to join old and new threads:

Make a loose loop.

After completing the next loop, pull the end of the old thread to fit.

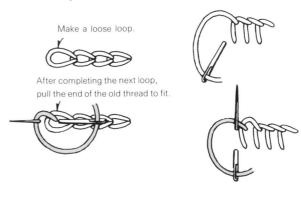

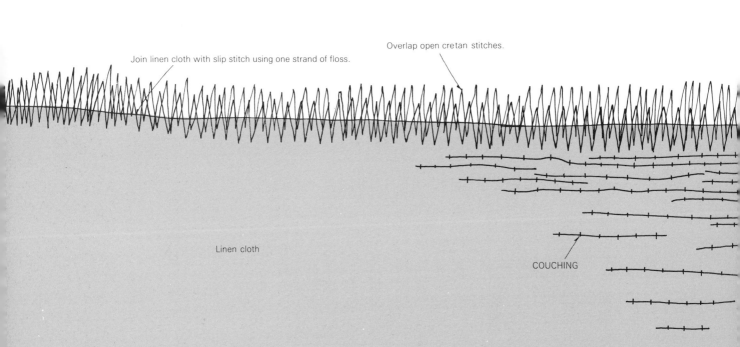

Join linen cloth with slip stitch using one strand of floss.

Overlap open cretan stitches.

Linen cloth

COUCHING

2

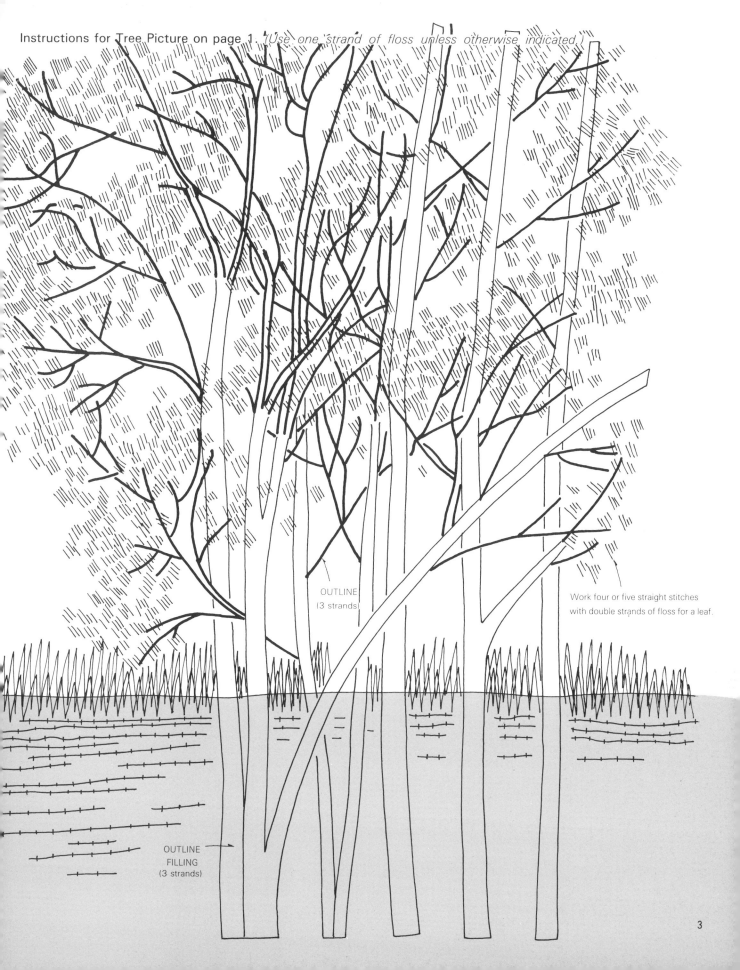

OUTLINE
(3 strands)

Work four or five straight stitches
with double strands of floss for a leaf.

OUTLINE
FILLING
(3 strands)

Town

Instructions on pages 6 & 7.

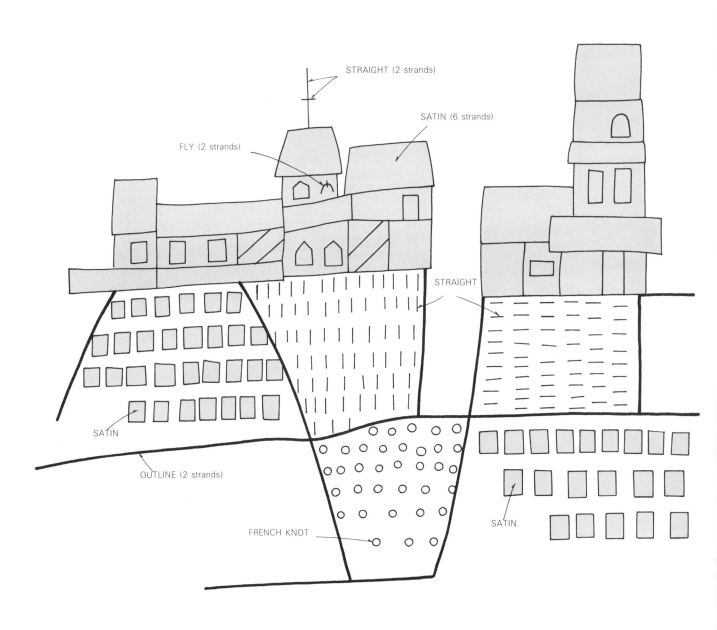

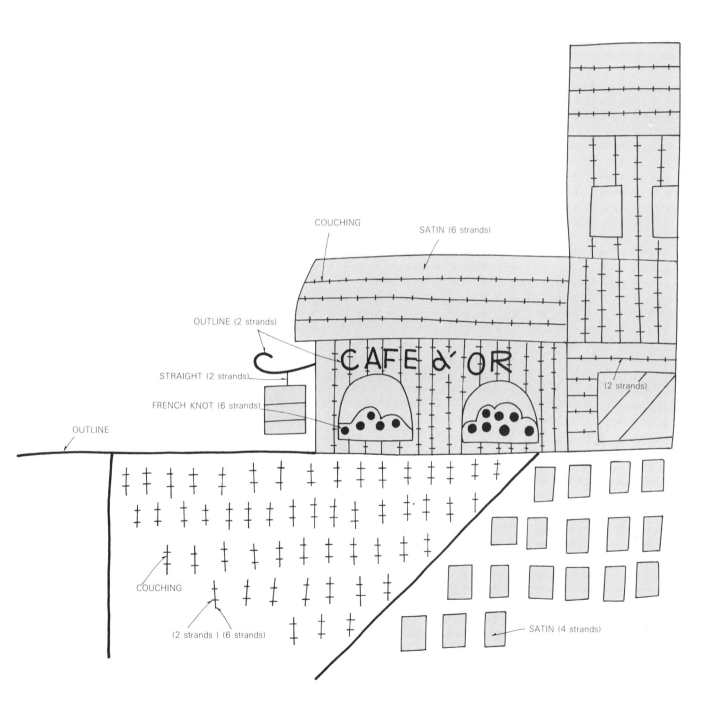

COUCHING

SATIN (6 strands)

OUTLINE (2 strands)

STRAIGHT (2 strands)

FRENCH KNOT (6 strands)

CAFE d'OR

(2 strands)

OUTLINE

COUCHING

(2 strands) (6 strands)

SATIN (4 strands)

Instructions on pages 10 & 11.

Instructions for Window on page 8. *(Use 3 strands of floss unless otherwise indicated.)*

Color bricks with quick dye referring to the photo on page 8.

OUTLINE

STRAIGHT

CHAIN FILLING

Gather top edge of curtain
and slip-stitch to window.

Sheeting

Cotton lace edging

FRENCH KNOT (2 strands)

CHAIN FILLING

OUTLINE FILLING

SATIN (2 strands)

STRAIGHT
(2 strands)

SATIN (2 strands)

LAZY DAISY

CHAIN FILLING

FRENCH KNOT (6 strands)

Instructions for Windows on page 9. *(Use 3 strands of floss unless otherwise indicated.)*

Color wall with quick dye
referring to the photo on page 9.

SATIN

OUTLINE

CHAIN

LONG &
SHORT

Tulle
Lace

FRENCH KNOT (6 strands)

LAZY DAIZY

CHAIN
FILLING

11

Breeze

Instructions on page 15.

13

Instructions for My Studio on page 12.

(Use 2 strands of floss unless otherwise indicated.)

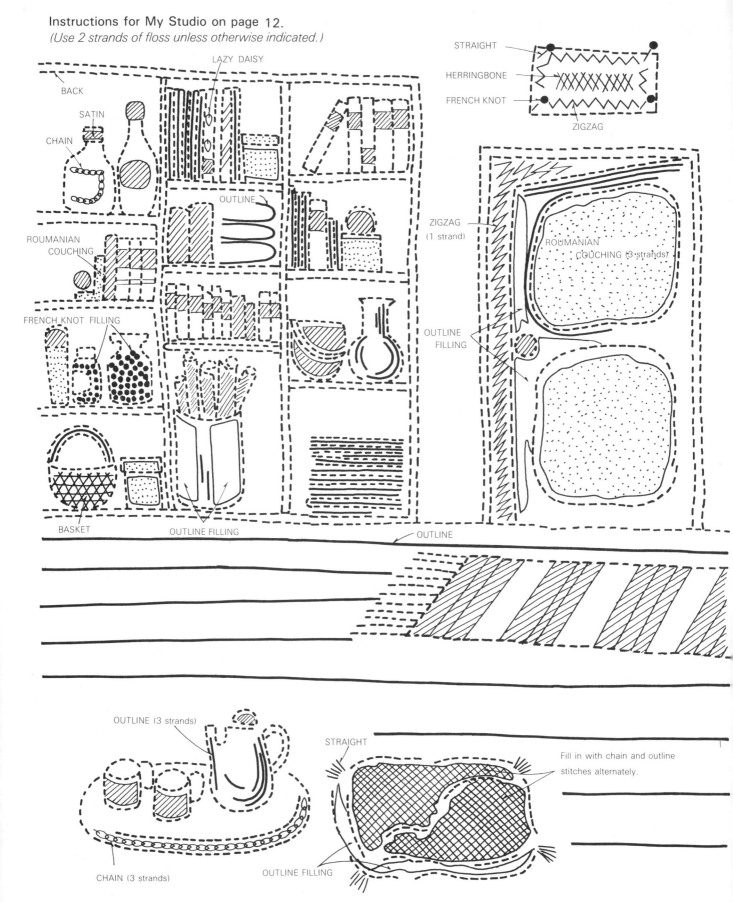

STRAIGHT

HERRINGBONE

FRENCH KNOT

ZIGZAG

BACK

LAZY DAISY

SATIN

CHAIN

OUTLINE

ROUMANIAN
COUCHING

ZIGZAG
(1 strand)

ROUMANIAN
COUCHING (3 strands)

FRENCH KNOT FILLING

OUTLINE
FILLING

BASKET

OUTLINE FILLING

OUTLINE

OUTLINE (3 strands)

STRAIGHT

Fill in with chain and outline
stitches alternately.

CHAIN (3 strands)

OUTLINE FILLING

14

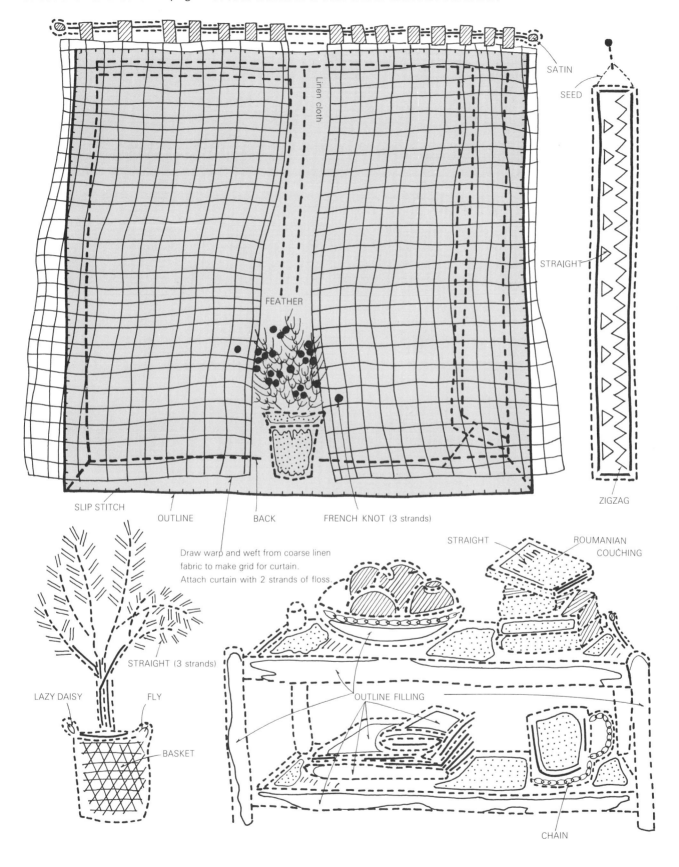

Linen cloth

SATIN

SEED

STRAIGHT

FEATHER

ZIGZAG

SLIP STITCH

OUTLINE

BACK

FRENCH KNOT (3 strands)

STRAIGHT

ROUMANIAN COUCHING

Draw warp and weft from coarse linen
fabric to make grid for curtain.
Attach curtain with 2 strands of floss.

STRAIGHT (3 strands)

OUTLINE FILLING

LAZY DAISY

FLY

BASKET

CHAIN

Four Seasons

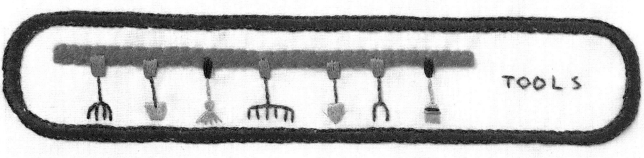

TOOLS

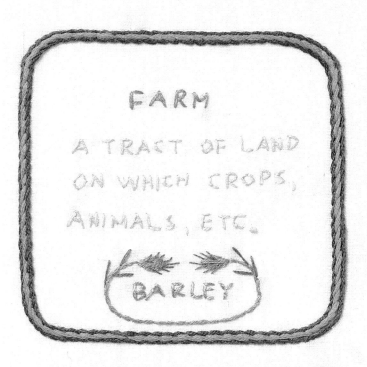

FARM

A TRACT OF LAND
ON WHICH CROPS,
ANIMALS, ETC.

BARLEY

AUTUMN

Instructions on pages 18 & 19.

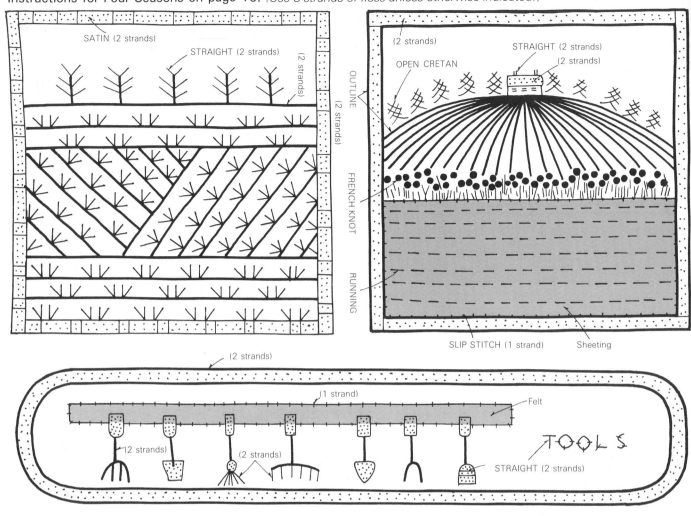

SATIN (2 strands)

STRAIGHT (2 strands)

(2 strands)

OUTLINE

(2 strands)

(2 strands)

OPEN CRETAN

STRAIGHT (2 strands)

(2 strands)

FRENCH KNOT

RUNNING

SLIP STITCH (1 strand)

Sheeting

(2 strands)

(1 strand)

Felt

(2 strands)

(2 strands)

TOOLS

STRAIGHT (2 strands)

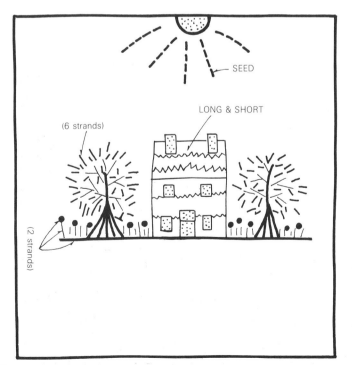

SEED

LONG & SHORT

(6 strands)

(2 strands)

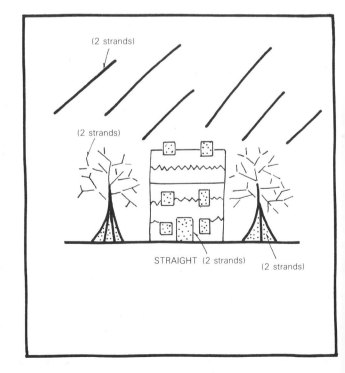

(2 strands)

(2 strands)

STRAIGHT (2 strands)

(2 strands)

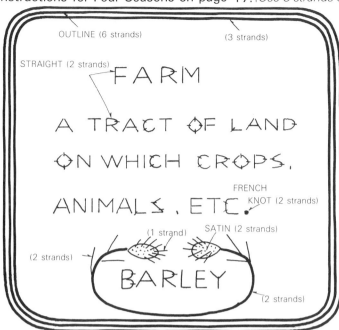

OUTLINE (6 strands)
(3 strands)
STRAIGHT (2 strands)

FARM

A TRACT OF LAND

ON WHICH CROPS,

ANIMALS, ETC.

FRENCH KNOT (2 strands)

(1 strand)   SATIN (2 strands)

(2 strands)

BARLEY

(2 strands)

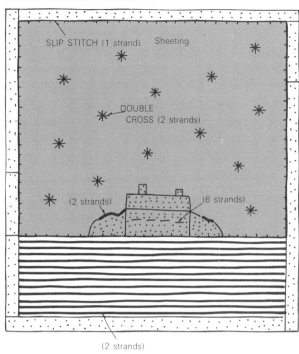

SLIP STITCH (1 strand)   Sheeting

DOUBLE CROSS (2 strands)

(2 strands)   (6 strands)

(2 strands)

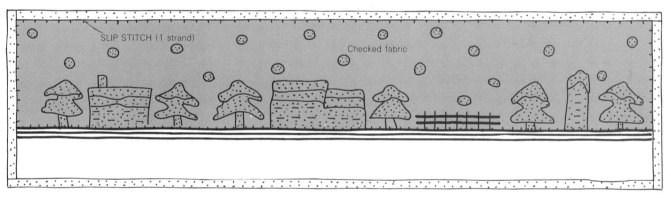

SLIP STITCH (1 strand)

Checked fabric

AUTUMN

FRENCH KNOT (6 strands)

(3 strands)

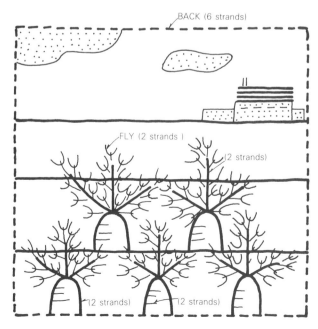

BACK (6 strands)

FLY (2 strands)

(2 strands)

(2 strands)   (2 strands)

19

Instructions on pages 22 & 23.

Instructions for Sweet Sixteen on page 20. *(Use 4 strands of floss unless otherwise indicated.)*

OUTLINE FILLING

BULLION (3 strands)

LONG & SHORT

OPEN BUTTONHOLE

SATIN (3 strands)

STRAIGHT (3 strands)

FLY VARIATION

BULLION

CHAIN FILLING

COUCHED TRELLIS

CHAIN (3 strands)

FLY VARIATION

CHAIN (3 strands)

OUTLINE

CHAIN

FLY

LAZY DAISY

SATIN (3 strands)

HERRINGBONE

SATIN (3 strands)

SATIN (3 strands)

22

Instructions for Sweet Sixteen on page 21. *(Use 4 strands of floss unless otherwise indicated.)*

OUTLINE FILLING

(3 strands)

SATIN (3 strands)

LONG & SHORT

(3 strands)

CHAIN (3 strands)

FLY

COUCHED TRELLIS

OUTLINE

FLY VARIATION

OPEN BUTTONHOLE

SATIN (3 strands)

FEATHER

LAZY DAISY

OUTLINE

(3 strands)

SATIN (3 strands)

Rabbit & Mole

Instructions on pages 26 & 27.

Instructions for Rabbit and Mole on pages 24 & 25.

(Embroider with 3 strands of floss and applique with one strand in slip stitch unless otherwise indicated.)

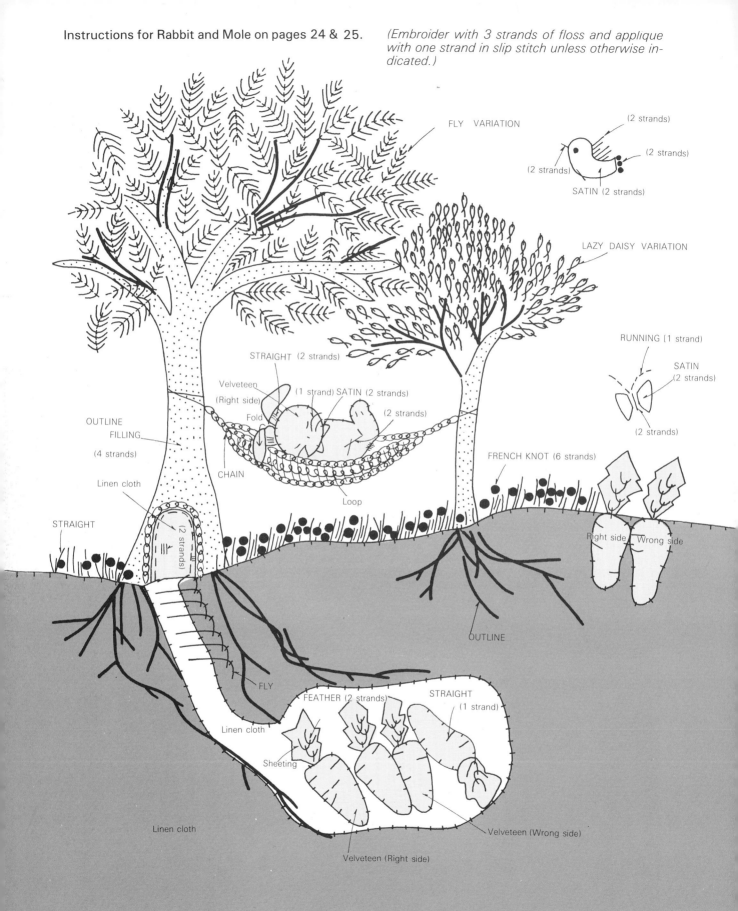

FLY VARIATION

(2 strands)

(2 strands)

(2 strands)

SATIN (2 strands)

LAZY DAISY VARIATION

RUNNING (1 strand)

SATIN (2 strands)

(2 strands)

STRAIGHT (2 strands)

Velveteen (Right side)

(1 strand) SATIN (2 strands)

(2 strands)

Fold

FRENCH KNOT (6 strands)

Right side   Wrong side

OUTLINE FILLING

(4 strands)

CHAIN

Loop

OUTLINE

Linen cloth

STRAIGHT

(2 strands)

FLY

FEATHER (2 strands)

STRAIGHT (1 strand)

Linen cloth

Sheeting

Velveteen (Wrong side)

Linen cloth

Velveteen (Right side)

26

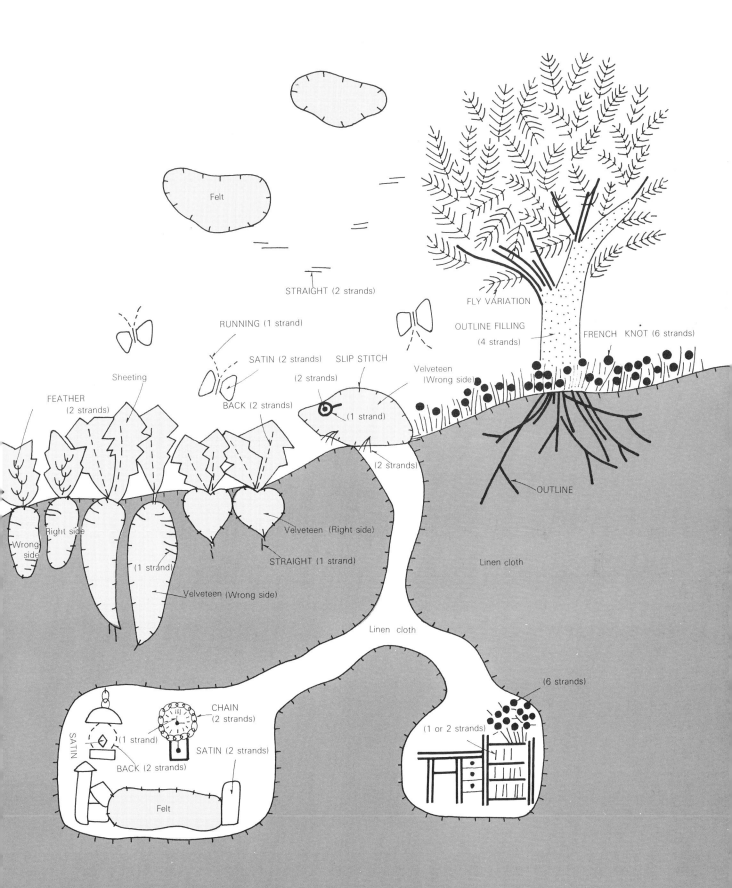

STRAIGHT (2 strands)

Felt

FLY VARIATION

OUTLINE FILLING
(4 strands)

FRENCH KNOT (6 strands)

RUNNING (1 strand)

SATIN (2 strands)

SLIP STITCH
(2 strands)

Velveteen
(Wrong side)

Sheeting

BACK (2 strands)

(1 strand)

FEATHER
(2 strands)

OUTLINE

(2 strands)

Right side

Wrong
side

Velveteen (Right side)

Linen cloth

(1 strand)

STRAIGHT (1 strand)

Velveteen (Wrong side)

Linen cloth

(6 strands)

CHAIN
(2 strands)

(1 strand)

(1 or 2 strands)

SATIN

SATIN (2 strands)

BACK (2 strands)

Felt

Good Night

Instructions on page 31.

Instructions for Good Night on page 28. *(Embroider with 2 strands of floss and applique with one strand unless otherwise indicated.)*

(3 strands).

SLIP STITCH

OUTLINE

STRAIGHT (1 strand)

(3 strands)

FRENCH KNOT

Tulle Lace

LAZY DAISY

STRAIGHT

Tulle Lace

Floral print

OUTLINE   FILLING (3 strands)

(3 strands)

(3 strands)

FLY (1 strand)

(3 strands)

(3 strands)

(1 strand)

(3 strands)

Cotton Lace edging

Green with dots

Cotton Broadcloth

(3 strands)

(3 strands)

(1 strand)

STRAIGHT

(3 strands)

CHAIN FILLING

SURFACE   DARNING   STITCH
(6 strands)

(2 strands)

30

Instructions for Spring on page 29. *(Embroider with 2 strands of floss and applique with one strand unless otherwise indicated.)*

SATIN.

CHAIN

RUNNING

OUTLINE FILLING (3 strands)

FRENCH KNOT

STRAIGHT (1 strand)

SLIP STITCH

Cotton Broadcloth

(6 strands)

(3 strands)

LAZY DAISY

FRENCH KNOT FILLING (3 strands)

(3 strands)

(3 strands)

FLY

(3 strands)

(3 strands)

(1 strand)

(3 strands)

(4 strands)

(3 strands)

(1 strand)

(3 strands)

(5 strands)

(4 strands)

(5 strands)

FEATHER

OUTLINE (5 strands)

OUTLINE FILLING (3 strands)

SATIN

Cotton Broadcloth

FRENCH KNOT FILLING (3 strands)

STRAIGHT (1 strand)

SLIP STITCH

LAZY DAISY

(3 strands)

(1 strand)

(3 strands)

(4 strands)

CH KNOT

STRAIGHT (1 strand)

(4 strands)

(5 strands)

STRAIGHT

(5 strands)

FEATHER

31

Flower Garden

Use 4 strands of floss unless otherwise indicated.

LAZY DAISY

SATIN (3 strands)

CHAIN FILLING (3 strands)

SURFACE DARNING

OUTLINE

STRAIGHT

FRENCH KNOT

STRAIGHT

SATIN (3 strands)

(3 strands)

(3 strands) (3 strands) (3 strands)

(3 strands)

(3 strands)

SATIN (3 strands)

CHAIN (3 strands)

(3 strands)

(3 strands)

LONG & SHORT

(3 strands)

DOUBLE LAZY DAISY

(3 strands)

(3 strands)

(3 strands)

FLY VARIATION (3 strands)

(6 strands)

(3 strands)

CORAL

(3 strands)

(3 strands)

(3 strands)

STRAIGHT

33

Use 3 strands of floss for satin and long & short stitches, and 4 strands for other stitches unless otherwise indicated.

LAZY DAISY

STRAIGHT

OUTLINE

STRAIGHT

CORAL

SATIN

CHAIN

LONG & SHORT

FRENCH KNOT

STRAIGHT

SATIN

(1 strand)

CHAIN FILLING

CHAIN FILLING

FLY

CHAIN FILLING

CHAIN FILLING

TWISTED CHAIN

OUTLINE FILLING

CHAIN FILLING

(3 strands)

CHAIN FILLING

STRAIGHT (2 strands)

CROSS

FLY

FRENCH KNOT (6 strands)

OUTLINE FILLING

COUCHED TRELLIS

Green Vegetables

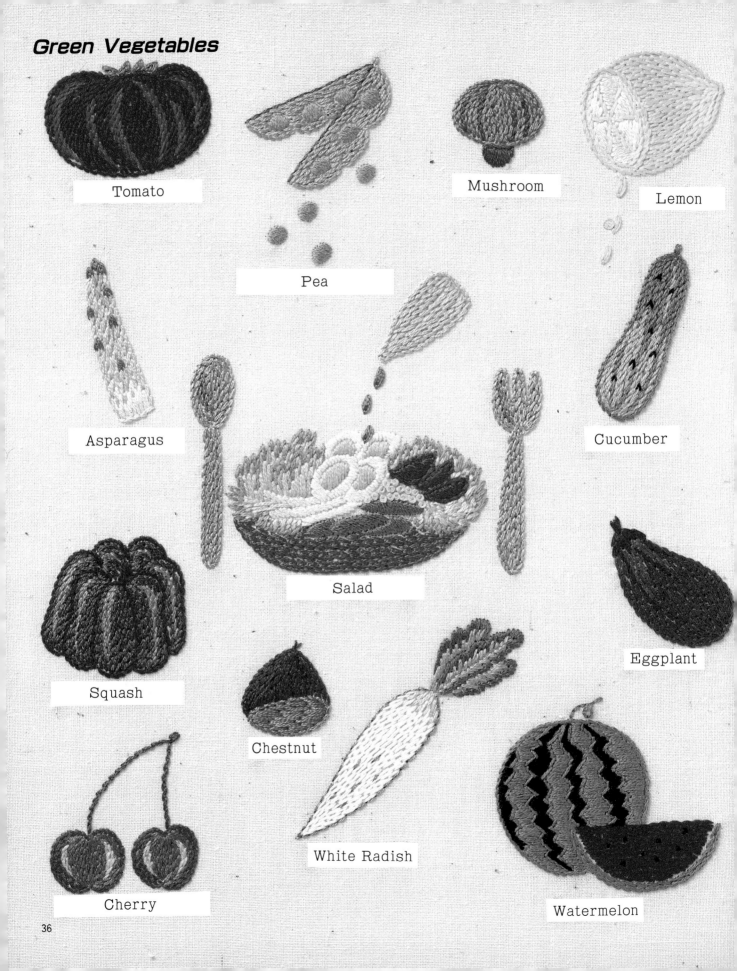

Tomato

Pea

Mushroom

Lemon

Asparagus

Cucumber

Salad

Squash

Chestnut

Eggplant

Cherry

White Radish

Watermelon

Use 3 strands of floss unless otherwise indicated.

STRAIGHT

OUTLINE

OUTLINE FILLING

BACK
(2 strands)

SATIN

LAZY DAISY

STRAIGHT

STRAIGHT

LONG & SHORT

LONG & SHORT

OUTLINE

SATIN

FRENCH KNOT FILLING

LONG & SHORT

SATIN

STRAIGHT

LONG & SHORT

STRAIGHT
(2 strands)

BACK

SATIN

ZIGZAG

STRAIGHT
(2 strands)

I like cooking

Embroider with 3 strands of floss and applique with 2 strands in slip stitch unless otherwise indicated.

CHAIN

OUTLINE (2 strands)

(2 strands)

SATIN

OPEN BUTTONHOLE

GERMAN KNOT

SATIN

LAZY DAISY

Bead

SATIN

FRENCH KNOT (2 strands)

(2 strands)

CROSS   STRAIGHT

Rickrack

SLIP STITCH

FRENCH KNOT (2 strands)

I like çooking

(2 strands)

STRAIGHT

STRAIGHT

BACK

SATIN

CHAIN FILLING

Picnic Lunch

Use 4 strands of floss unless otherwise indicated.

OUTLINE

OUTLINE FILLING

(3 strands)

CHAIN FILLING
(3 strands)

FLY
(3 strands)

STRAIGHT
SATIN
(3 strands)

(3 strands)

LUNCH

FRENCH   KNOT
(2 strands)

SANDWICH

CHAIN

(3 strands)

LONG & SHORT (3 strands)

LAZY DAISY

OPEN BUTTONHOLE

CORAL

DOUBLE CROSS

(3 strands)

STRAIGHT

COUCHED
TRELLIS

FRENCH
KNOT

COUCHED TRELLIS

(3 strands)

STRAIGHT
(3 strands)

(3 strands)

ZIGZAG

41

KENTA

COUCHING (1 strand)
Cotton à broder
(2 strands)
BACK
OUTLINE FILLING

SATIN

OUTLINE
SATIN (2 strands)
LONG & SHORT (2 strands)
(1 strand)
(2 strands)
Checked fabric

Cotton Broadcloth
SLIP STITCH

12
9
3
6
STRAIGHT
CHAIN FILLING
(2 strands)

KENTA
(2 strands)

(2 strands)

SATIN

(2 strands)
(2 strands)
(2 strands)
SATIN
(2 strands)
SATIN
LONG & SHORT

SATIN
(2 strands)

FRENCH KNOT (2 strands)
(1 strand)
A
(2 strands)
(2 strands)
(2 strands)

akira

keiko

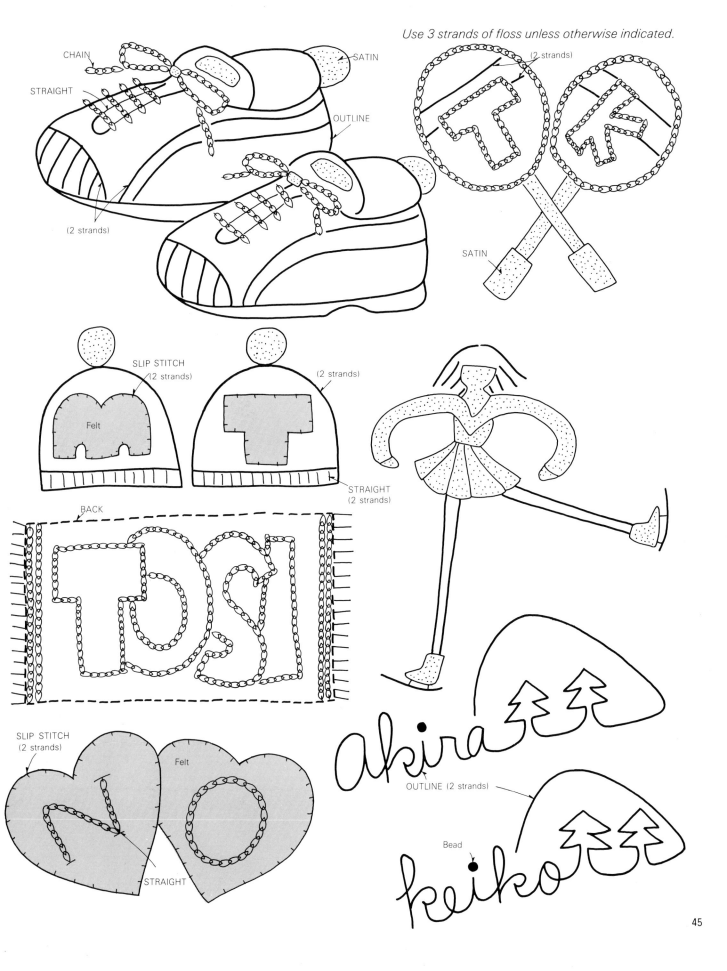

CHAIN

STRAIGHT

SATIN

OUTLINE

(2 strands)

Use 3 strands of floss unless otherwise indicated.

(2 strands)

SATIN

SLIP STITCH
(2 strands)

(2 strands)

Felt

STRAIGHT
(2 strands)

BACK

SLIP STITCH
(2 strands)

Felt

STRAIGHT

akira

OUTLINE (2 strands)

Bead

keiko

Embroider with 2 strands of floss and applique with one strand in open buttonhole stitch.

OUTLINE

OUTLINE FILLING

Felt

OPEN BUTTONHOLE

CHAIN

STRAIGHT (1 strand)

ball

SATIN

OUTLINE (1 strand)

STRAIGHT

LAZY DAISY

FRENCH KNOT

(1 strand)

SATIN

STRAIGHT

STRAIGHT (1 strand)

SLIP STITCH (1 strand)

Color cheeks with a colored pencil.

CHAIN FILLING

STRAIGHT   Thread 2 beads and stitch.

CHAIN FILLING

OUTLINE (3 strands)

FRENCH KNOT (3 strands)

OUTLINE

Lets

Felt

Color cheeks with a colored pencil.

OUTLINE (1 strand)

SKI!

FLY (3 strands)

CHAIN (3 strands)

OPEN BUTTONHOLE (3 strands)

RANDOM CROSS (4 strands)

FLY

CHAIN

FRENCH KNOT

1

SATIN

OUTLINE

STRAIGHT   Thread 2 beads and stitch.

OUTLINE FILLING

CHAIN FILLING

RANDOM CROSS

STRAIGHT

SATIN (3 strands)

BETA

Use 3 strands of floss and one strand of lamé thread unless otherwise indicated.

FRENCH KNOT

FLY

SATIN

OUTLINE

my treasures

BACK (2 strands)

BACK

FLY VARIATION

CHAIN

Bead

STRAIGHT

LAZY DAISY

BULLION CHAIN

OUTLINE FILLING

Spangle

Bead

ZIGZAG

OPEN BUTTONHOLE

STRAIGHT

A

SEED FILLING

OUTLINE
(2 strands)

BETA

Unique Emblems

OUTLINE — LONG & SHORT

Cotton Broadcloth

SATIN

LONG & SHORT

LAZY DAISY

OUTLINE (3 strands)

ZIGZAG
OUTLINE
FILLING

CHAIN

MUSIC

LONG & SHORT
(3 strands)

LOVER

SURFACE DARNING
(6 strands)

SATIN

OUTLINE
(3 strands)

SATIN

ART

STRAIGHT

SATIN

SEED (3 strands)

HITOMI

SATIN
(3 strands)

MASATO

SATIN

OUTLINE FILLING
(3 strands)

SATIN
(3 strands)

(3 strands)

Cycling

FOLK SONG

SATIN

OUTLINE

Cotton
Broadcloth

SATIN

SATIN (3 strands)

OUTLINE SATIN (3 strands)

LONG & SHORT
(3 strands)

RFC

STRAIGHT
(4 strands)

Embroider with 2 strands of floss and applique with one strand in slip stitch unless otherwise indicated.

Materials for Cosmetic Case:

Quilted fabric: Blue gingham checks, 33cm by 27cm ($13^{1}/_{4}'' \times 10^{3}/_{4}''$); unbleached, 18cm by 14cm ($7^{1}/_{4}'' \times 5^{5}/_{8}''$). Navy cotton broadcloth, 46cm by 23.5cm ($18^{3}/_{8}'' \times 9^{5}/_{8}''$).

DMC six strand embroidery floss, No. 25: Small amount each of mahogany (301), umber (437), royal blue (996, 796) and black (310). Navy zipper, 20cm ($8''$) long. Navy piping tape, 110cm ($44''$) long.

Directions

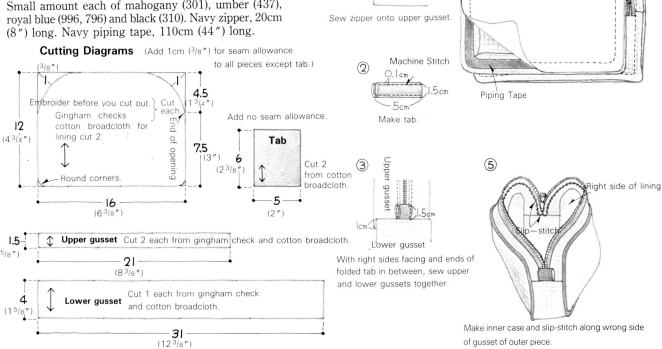

Cutting Diagrams (Add 1cm ($^{3}/_{8}''$) for seam allowance to all pieces except tab.)

① Sew zipper onto upper gusset.
Machine Stitch 0.2cm / 1cm / 1.5cm

② Make tab.
Machine Stitch 0.1cm / 1.5cm / 5cm

③ With right sides facing and ends of folded tab in between, sew upper and lower gussets together.
Upper gusset / Lower gusset / 1.5cm / 1cm

④ With right sides facing, sew front and gusset together.
Piping Tape

⑤ Make inner case and slip-stitch along wrong side of gusset of outer piece.
Right side of lining / Slip–stitch

Cutting Diagrams:
Embroider before you cut out. Gingham checks cotton broadcloth for lining cut 2. Round corners.
Cut each / End of opening
12 ($4^{3}/_{4}''$) / 16 ($6^{3}/_{8}''$) / 4.5 ($1^{3}/_{4}''$) / 7.5 ($3''$) / ($^{3}/_{8}''$)

Add no seam allowance.
Tab Cut 2 from cotton broadcloth.
6 ($2^{3}/_{8}''$) / 5 ($2''$)

Upper gusset Cut 2 each from gingham check and cotton broadcloth.
1.5 ($^{5}/_{8}''$) / 21 ($8^{3}/_{8}''$)

Lower gusset Cut 1 each from gingham check and cotton broadcloth.
4 ($1^{5}/_{8}''$) / 31 ($12^{3}/_{8}''$)

Handmade Cards

Embroider with 2 strands of floss and applique with one strand in open buttonhole stitch.

Felt

OUTLINE

RANDOM CROSS

Attach felt with bead

Straight-stitch on felt.

(1 strand)

STRAIGHT
Thread 2 beads and stitch.

CHAIN FILLING

FLY
(1 strand)

Bead

Spangle

(3 strands)

(4 strands)

(3 strands)

STRAIGHT
(1 strand)

LAZY DAISY

FLY

CHAIN
Take two stitches and tie ends into bow.

STRAIGHT
(1 strand)

CHAIN FILLING

OPEN BUTTONHOLE

OUTLINE

CHAIN
(3 strands)

OUTLINE

SATIN

STRAIGHT

RANDOM CROSS

CHAIN FILLING

Color cheeks with a colored pencil.

(1 strand)

SATIN

CHAIN

(1 strand)

OUTLINE FILLING

STRAIGHT
(1 strand)

SATIN

LAZY DAISY

CHAIN FILLING

52

Materials for Cards: *See page 52 for colors of felt.*

	Patterns	DMC six strand embroidery floss, No. 25	Beads	Cardboard
LOVE	Yellow green 11.5 cm by 10 cm (4⁵⁄8″ × 4″). Scraps of pink and cherry pink.	Small amount each of geranium pink (891), magenta rose (963), plum (553), golden yellow (782) and white.	Black (Small) 4 pieces	Soft pink 3.5 cm by 15 cm (14″ × 6″)
BABY	Light blue 12 cm square (4³⁄4″). Scraps of cherry pink.	Small amount each of soft pink (819), geranium pink (891), light yellow (3078, 782) and black (310).	Pink 3 pieces	Soft pink 28.5 cm by 16.5 cm (11³⁄8″ × 6⁵⁄8″).
For FRESHMAN	Soft pink 15.5 cm by 16 cm (6¹⁄4″ × 6³⁄8″). Scraps of yellow green.	Small amount each of mahogany (301), brilliant green (704), poppy (666) and forget-me-not blue (825).	Black (Small) 2 pieces	While 17.5 cm by 33.5 cm (7″ × 13³⁄8″).

Actual-size   Cut out letters from felt and glue to cards.

How to make card

Cut out desired shape from 2 sheets of cardboard and make a window in first piece. Fit embroidered felt in the window and fix with glue. Glue second piece onto wrong side of first piece.

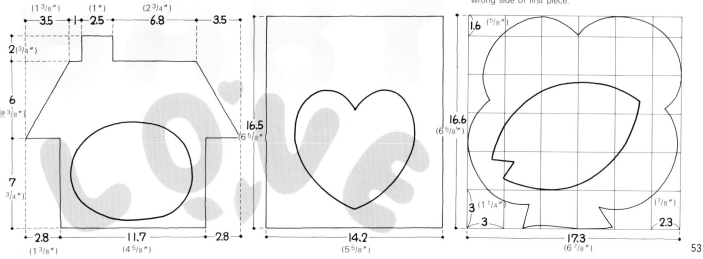

Cosmetic Cases

SATIN

OUTLINE

CHAIN FILLING

(2 strands)

CROSS
(2 strands) BACK

SATIN

(2 strands)

COUCHING
(6 strands)

(1 strand)

OUTLINE

a day's
journey

STRAIGHT
(4 strands)

SATIN

SEED FILLING

OPEN
BUTTONHOLE

CHAIN
FILLING

FRENCH
KNOT

OUTLINE
FILLING

OUTLINE
FILLING

SATIN

SEED
FILLING

(1 strand)

SATIN

STRAIGHT

OUTLINE FILLING

(2 strands)

STRAIGHT

OUTLINE

SATIN
(2 strands)

FLY
VARIATION

FLY

Spangle

Bead

BACK
(2 strands)

54

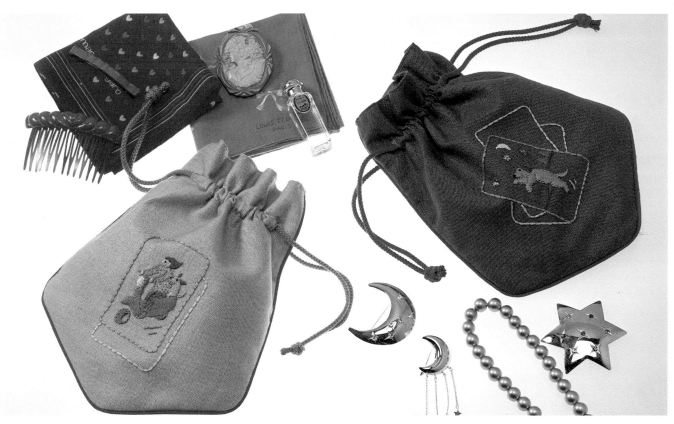

Materials for Cosmetic Cases:

Linen fabric: Ocher for Ⓐ and navy for Ⓑ, 56cm by 19cm ($22^{3}/8'' \times 7^{5}/8''$) each.

Sheeting: Same color with linen for Ⓐ and Ⓑ, 36cm by 19cm ($14^{3}/8'' \times 7^{5}/8''$).

Cutting Diagrams
(Add 0.5cm ($^{1}/4''$) all around for seam allowance.)

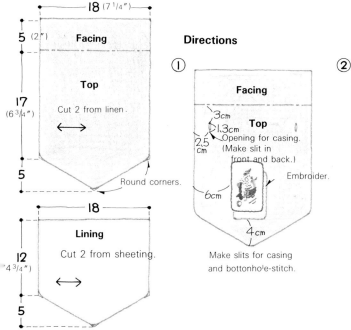

18 ($7^{1}/4''$)

5 (2")

Facing

Top
Cut 2 from linen.

17 ($6^{3}/4''$)

5

Round corners.

18

Lining
Cut 2 from sheeting.

12 ($4^{3}/4''$)

5

Directions

① **Facing**

3cm
1.3cm
2.5 cm
Opening for casing.
(Make slit in front and back.)

Top

Embroider.

6cm

4cm

Make slits for casing and bottonho!e-stitch.

DMC six strand embroidery floss, No. 25:
For Ⓐ:Small amount each of magenta rose(963), geranium pink (893), cerise (605, 602), parma violet (208), plum (552), royal blue (996), ash gray (414), apricot pink (951), golden yellow (783), umber gold (975), lemon yellow (445), canary yellow (971), black (310) and white; For Ⓑ:Small amount each of magenta rose(963), geranium pink (893), cerise (605, 602), plum (550), parma violet (209), ash gray (762), umber gold (975), golden yellow (783), lemon yellow (445) and black (310). Red piping tape for Ⓐ and Ⓑ, 65.5cm ($26^{1}/4''$) each.

Cotton cord: Light brown for Ⓐ and navy for Ⓑ, 0.4cm ($^{1}/8''$) in diameter and 104cm ($41^{5}/8''$) long. Star-shaped spangles and beads for Ⓑ, 3 each.

② Opening for turning.
Lining Wrong side
With right sides facing, sew linen and sheeting together. Turn seams to linen.

Facing

Top Wrong side
With right sides facing and piping tape in between, sew two pieces together leaving top open for turning.

Insert 52cm ($20^{3}/4''$)-long cord into casing of front and back pieces.

③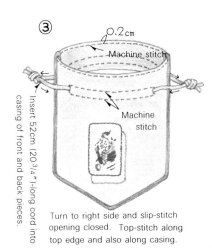

0.2 cm
Machine stitch

Machine stitch

Turn to right side and slip-stitch opening closed. Top-stitch along top edge and also along casing.

55

Placemat Appliques

Use 3 strands of floss unless otherwise indicated. Cut out applique pieces adding 0.3 cm all around for seam allowance and slop-stitch with 2 strands of floss.

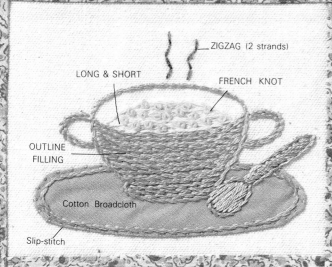

ZIGZAG (2 strands)
FRENCH KNOT
LONG & SHORT
OUTLINE FILLING
Cotton Broadcloth
Slip-stitch

STRAIGHT (2 strands)
SATIN
BACK (2 strands)
PEPPER SALT

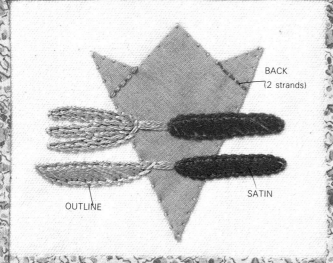

BACK (2 strands)
OUTLINE
SATIN
OUTLINE

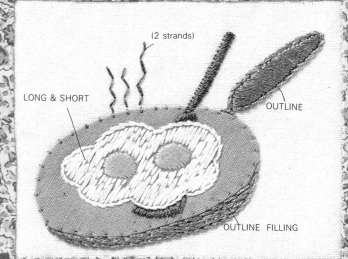

(2 strands)
LONG & SHORT
OUTLINE
OUTLINE FILLING

OUTLINE
LONG & SHORT
ZIGZAG (2 strands)

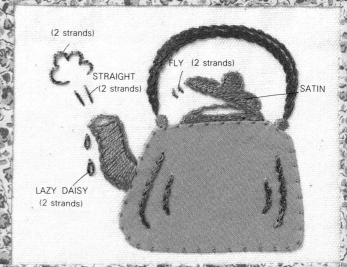

(2 strands)
STRAIGHT (2 strands)
FLY (2 strands)
SATIN
LAZY DAISY (2 strands)

56

Materials for placemats:

For Placemat with olive-green print: Unbleached canvas, 48cm by 34.5cm ($19\frac{1}{4}'' \times 13\frac{3}{4}''$). Olive-green print, 42cm by 20cm($16\frac{3}{4}'' \times 8''$).

Cutting Diagram

Canvas

34.5
($13\frac{3}{4}''$)

Seam allowance

48
($19\frac{1}{4}''$)

34.5

Cotton print

20
(8")

Seam allowance

5
(2")

42
($16\frac{3}{4}''$)

Fold seam allowance of canvas to right side. Fold seam allowance of print to wrong side and place on canvas with edges even.

Directions

① 3 — 42

($\frac{3}{8}''$) Baste

Canvas

3

② Slip-stitch

Baste

3 ($1\frac{1}{4}''$)

DMC six strand embroidery floss, No. 25: Small amount each of ash gray (317, 414, 415), black (310), tangerine yellow (742) and white.

Fabric for applique: Scraps of gray, mustard and lavender cotton fabric.

For Placemat with rose pink print: Unbleached canvas, 48cm by 34.5cm ($19\frac{1}{4}'' \times 13\frac{3}{4}''$). Rose pink print, 42cm by 20cm ($16\frac{3}{4}'' \times 8''$).

DMC six strand embroidery floss, No. 25: Small amount each of violet mauve (327), episcopal purple (718), parma violet (209), ash gray (415, 318), golden yellow (781), turkey red (321) and green (3052).

Fabric for applique: Scraps of mauve and beige cotton fabric.

③
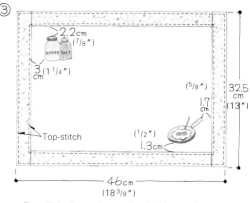

2.2cm ($\frac{7}{8}''$)

3cm ($1\frac{1}{4}''$)

($\frac{5}{8}''$)

32.5 cm (13")

1.7 cm

Top-stitch

($\frac{1}{2}''$)

1.3cm

46cm ($18\frac{3}{8}''$)

Top-stitch along edges and embroider as shown.

OUTLINE

STRAIGHT

SATIN

FRENCH KNOT

SATIN

OUTLINE

SATIN

STRAIGHT

SATIN

BACK

FRENCH KNOT
(1 strand)

OUTLINE
(1 strand)

(3 strands)

DARNING (3 strands)

LONG & SHORT

CROSS

STRAIGHT

SATIN

STRAIGHT

DOUBLE LAZY DAISY

SATIN

FLY
(1 strand)

FRENCH
KNOT

STRAIGHT

OUTLINE

LAZY DAISY

FLY

RUNNING

LAZY DAISY VARIATION

BACK

Use 2 strands of floss unless otherwise indicated.

Bib (Embroidery Area)

Use ready-made bib of
19.5cm by 22cm (7³/₄″ × 8³/₄″).

1.9
cm
(7⁵/₈″)

(826)
(704)
(988)
(913)
(794) white
White (891)
(644)
(796) (498)
(988) (1³/₄″)
(11⁵/₈″)
29cm
4.5cm
(434) 4.5 (794) (839)
cm

Numbers in parentheses indicate colors of DMC six strand
embroidery floss, No. 25.

Handkerchief

Embroidery Area and Designs

(Actual Size)

Use 33cm(13¹/₄″)-square
gauze handkerchiefs.

Design for B
(Embroider
at three corners.)

1.8cm
(³/₄″)

2.3cm
(⁷/₈″)

Design for A (Embroider at one corner.)

1.8cm

(444)
(310)
(445)
(913)
(498)

1.8cm

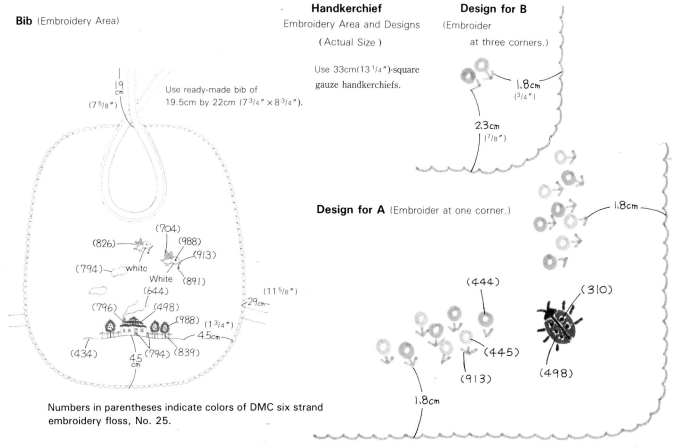

BASIC EMBROIDERY STITCHES

Straight stitch

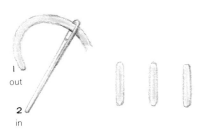

Running Stitch

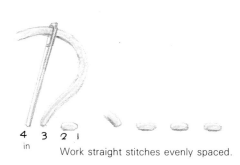

Work straight stitches evenly spaced.

Open Buttonhole Stitch

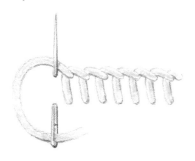

Back Stitch

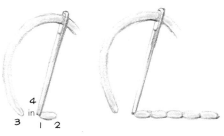

Work backward stitches evenly.

Seed Stitch

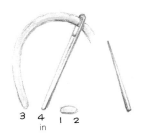

Work half back stitches

Seed Filling Stitch

Fill in the area with seed stitches regularly or freely.

Outline Stitch

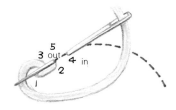

Outline Filling Stitch

Fill in the area with outline stitches.

Coral Stitch

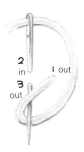

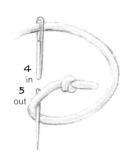

Random Cross Stitch

Work straight stitches in different length freely.

60

Couching

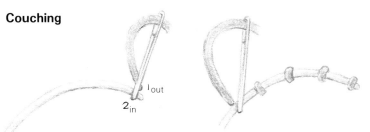

Tie down the laid thread with small stitches at right angles.

Roumanian Couching

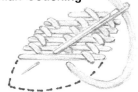

Lay thread lengthwise and tie down with slant stitches.

Chain Stitch

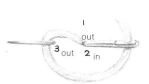

Chain Filling Stitch

Finish with a small stitch.

Fill in the area with chain stitches.

Twisted Chain Stitch

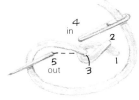

Lazy Daisy Stitch

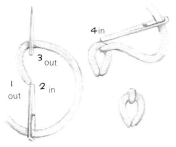

Double Lazy Daisy Stitch

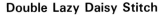
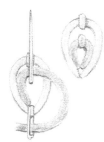

Work smaller stitch inside larger stitch.

Lazy Daisy Stitch Variation

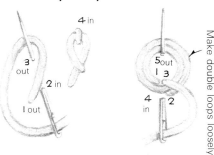

Make double loops loosely.

Bullion Stitch

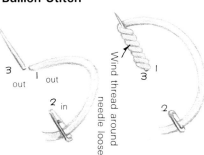

Wind thread around needle loosely.

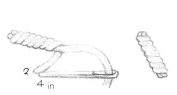

Pull needle through and turn back to insert at 4, next to starting point.

Bullion Chain Stitch

Wind thread around needle to make longer coil.

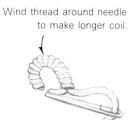

Pull Needle through and turn back to insert at starting point.

French Knot

French Knot Filling

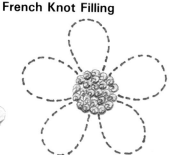

Fill in with French knots.

German Knot

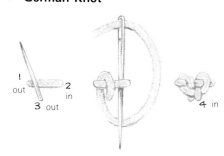

Fly Stitch

  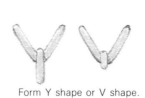

Form Y shape or V shape.

Fly Stitch Variation

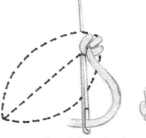 

Work fly stitches closely spaced.

Feather Stitch.

 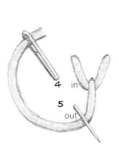 

Open Cretan Stitch

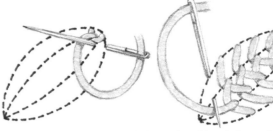

Work as for feather stitch, but make wider stitches to left and right sides alternately.

Herringbone Stitch

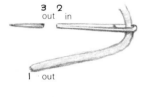 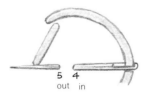 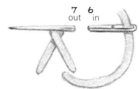 

Zigzag Stitch

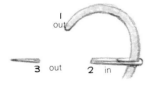 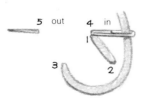 

Cross Stitch

Double Cross Stitch

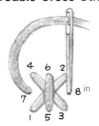

Work another cross stitch over cross stitch.

Loop Stitch

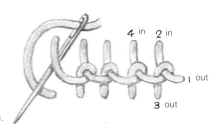

Satin Stitch

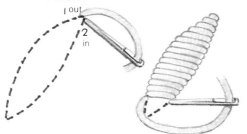

Long and Short Stitch

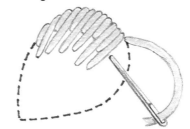

Basket Stitch

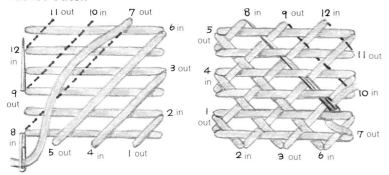

Surface Darning Stitch

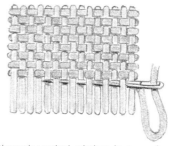

Pass thread through vertical stitches in a regular over and under sequence.

Couched Trellis Stitch

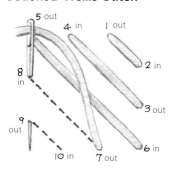
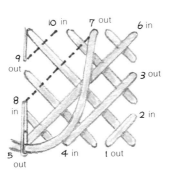

Tie each crossed thread down with a small stitch.

After tying with horizontal stitches, tie with vertical stitches to make cross.

Applique: Applique means applying or attaching another piece of fabric, leather or lace cut into desired shapes onto a background fabric with stitches or glue. This is also called Applied work. Closely woven fabric like felt which does not fray easily is suitable for applique. Choose the most suitable fabric for the background. Add 0.3—0.5cm ($1/8"$ — $1/4"$) for seam allowance except felt and leather which do not need seam allowance. Transfer designs onto background fabric, attach applique pieces with glue or basting stitches, then applique with desired thread and stitches.

Open butttonhole Stitch

Pieces without seam allowance are attached with this stitch.

Slip Stitch

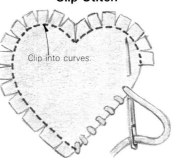

Slip-stitch at right angles with the folded edge showing very little stitches.